Material Support

EAMONN LYNSKEY

Published in 2023 by
Salmon Poetry
Cliffs of Moher, County Clare, Ireland
Website: www.salmonpoetry.com
Email: info@salmonpoetry.com

ISBN 978-1-915022-32-5

Biblical quotations are from *The New Jerusalem Bible* (Doubleday Standard Edition, 1999)

Cover Photography: *'Rossbeigh Beach, near Killorglin, Co. Kerry' by Martin Jakubik, EirLandscape.com*
Cover Design & Typesetting: *Siobhán Hutson*
Printed in Ireland by Sprint Print

Salmon Poetry gratefully acknowledges the support of The Arts Council / An Chomhairle Ealaíon

*In memory of John Wallace
poet, teacher, scholar and good friend*

Contents

A Poem Must

A poem must

depart the hand created it,
break free from all constraints, deny
all ties, all antecedents, be
the lever shifts the stone aside,

reveals the moment come for those
with ears will hear, with eyes will see—
a poem must be radiant
despite the darkness nurtured it,

be kind despite the pain endured,
must suffer its gethsemanes
alone, become insistent presence
haunting busy thoroughfares,

waylaying hurried figures trapped
in daily business—this one trading
in his shop or that one working
in his field will plead excuses,

turn away but turn again,
will feel a strange paralysis
afflict him, sense beneath the rib
an exultation flood the soul.

I

The mind sees the world as a thing apart,
And the soul makes the world at one with itself …

EDGAR LEE MASTERS

He Walks His Several Cities

Solo nella tradizione è il mio amore
—Pier Paolo Pasolini

Lost again, he walks his several cities,
stranger among strangers, hearing tongues
that speak a language recognisable
though suffused with unfamiliar phrases.

Moving always between past and present
and then back again, he makes his way
along new-tarmaced roads and new-laid pavements,
seeing cobblestones and alleyways

that once had led to busy Viking wharfs.
The Liffey's acrid stench—long-gone—assails him
and the river at low tide reveals
old mooring posts and ghosts of Guinness barges.

In the narrow medieval lanes
that wind through Temple Bar he finds a maze
of little Jewish garment factories
instead of restaurants and pizzerias,

all the weedy derelicts he knew
replaced by gleaming chrome and glass; the junk shops,
pawn shops, musty book shops vanished;
churches—open all day once—now closed.

And it's the Pillar, not the Spire, he sees—
remembering the long climb up to stand
between the seagulls and the Admiral
to view the distant Corporation Housing

built to clear the tenements and slums
romanticised through story, song and stage,
but screened from view when Queen Victoria
rode her regal cart down Sackville Street

before this pocket city of the Empire
crumbled into insignificant remnants
of imperial grandeur and became
a 1950s transit point for emigrants.

Unhappy times, yet he's nostalgic now
and even for the hardships, comforted
that Smith O'Brien, O'Connell, and Sir John Grey
stand resolute on their pedestals as yet;

Cuchullain still convulsed in epic struggle,
constable Sheahan's bravery remembered
at Burgh Quay—these stubborn survivors
offer compass through refurbished streets

where he is like a snail with house on back,
where he is like a book now out of print,
where he is like a refugee who cannot
shed the memory of what he's lost.

The more he walks the bustling streets the more
he feels a spectre, part of a Malton scene
where well-dressed gentry stroll pet dogs across
a wide, almost deserted, College Green

or trapped in some old sepia print of crowds
that blur on thoroughfares of trams and drays
and he's the only figure standing hesitant,
uncertain, wondering is it safe to cross.

Leeson Street Bridge, Evening

Impatient at the red light on the bridge
they crowd the kerb, grudge every moment lost,
frustrated at the tiniest subtraction
from the hours allowed them turn their backs
on weekly stats, accounts-due, invoices
and office politics. There is a time

to kill the flickering screen, adjust the eye
to open-plan of streets, remark the crease
a swan leaves in its wake. There is a time
to latch the door, throw off the coat and try
to resurrect a semblance of the self—

the lights are green again. The time is now.

Side Street

from The Hiding Place
by Tom Duddy (1950-2012)
published by Arlen House, 2011

I don't often pass through this part of the city,
though it's on my way uptown as the crow flies.
I don't feel at home here, or streetwise - it's cold,
even when the sun is warming the chimneys,

and dark to boot. My footsteps lose their beat,
the paths are so skewed, so irregular here.
The people are not the same as mainstreet people—
a woman comes dashing out of the shoe repair

(Heels-While-U-Wait) shop and cries *Sorry*; pieces
of burnt paper float from somewhere behind me,
and the man loping rapidly ahead of me
without looking back shouts *Shag off, will ye!*

(but not angrily) at some guys just out of range
of the corner of my eye. They say nothing at all,
these guys, as the loper increases his lead,
nor do they overtake me. The hot sharp smell

of burnt paper darts to the back of my throat,
and I think a small fragment, like a green flake
of distemper from the wall of an old porch,
has landed on my shoulder, but I can't check

or be seen to brush it off. Stepping into mainstreet
is like returning through the looking-glass without
a moment's notice—shoppers tucked in behind me,
not a thing on my shoulder, slight catch in my throat.

by kind permission, Arlen House

Remembering Tom Duddy

You could have chosen other streets
to write about: wide shopping plazas
loud with buskers, crowds and colour

but instead you chose a street
out of the usual tread, so cold
and dark to boot despite the sunshine.

And its people, *not the same
as mainstreet people*, seemed to have
an otherworldly air about them,

phantoms trapped in middle ground
between the present here-we-have
and the mysterious hereafter,

where the ordinary is up-ended
and the *skewed, irregular*
and extra-ordinary is the norm.

But where to find it now, your street
of wonderous inhabitations?
Now you've stepped into its paths

irrevocably, left no directions—
fragmentary descriptions, yes—
but no co-ordinates to help me.

There are times I walk this city
tempted to turn down this lane
or that secluded byway, thinking

here I'll meet you walking towards me,
brace of newly purchased books
held underarm, your hand outstretched.

The Where

Late that evening and her bus missed
and no lift, she hitch-hiked straight
into oblivion, left no rumour,
clue, no fingerprint, not smallest
faintest trace of her departure.

Unremarkable that day
that dawned like any other but
a mainstay in its superstructure
didn't hold— a bolt came loose,
a strut, a fret inched out of place

or if it be that happenings
are mapped out for the best beforehand,
something cloven intervened
to turn her step out of the path
ordained to guide her safely home.

How hard the waiting year on year
the doorbell, phone bell, feel the sorrow
welling in the throat until
we come to hope to hear the words
we never thought we'd hope to hear.

And darker than the deed itself
the heart that hides it, will not tell
the how, the where, the when. The where
is all that matters now. What bog?
What brambled mountainside? What fen?

Remembrance Day

'When there was peace, he was for peace:
when there was war, he went'

W. H. AUDEN

How to check the desperation
floods the heart to see these graves
so many new among the old?
And how persuade the mason carve
the less of selfless sacrifice,
the more of lives destroyed?

> *New epitaphs*
> *are needed,*

words might tell the gap was left
by those who went without demur
who might have spent their fruitful years
at work in these surrounding farms
instead of lying here so soon
among ancestral kin.

> *New epitaphs*
> *are needed,*

words would stand alongside dates
of inconclusive wars—Korea,
Vietnam—might tell of those
that fell, and tell of those they felled
and sent to fill the endless lists
of history's innocents.

> *New epitaphs*
> *are needed,*

for these headstones decorated
with star-spangled pennants—words
might cause a mourner think of fields
far distant under foreign skies
that yield a self-same crop of stone
this cold November morning.

Vermont, USA

19

Black Saturday 1941 Revisited

Greyfriars church destroyed,
she tells us. Pater Noster too ...
   A challenge to both sides:
   the one to carry out
   its most destructive Blitz.
   The other to come through,
   still fighting. War, you know...

Inside the ruined walls
we listen to the past ...
   A Nazi bomber reached
   the Palace but was downed
   by one of our brave pilots.
   He survived. Unfortunately,
   the bomber crew did not ...

She shows the shrapnel damage,
jagged, unrepaired ...
   so we will all remember
   how our city suffered.
   How other cities fared ...
   but we must leave all that
   behind us and ... move on.

And one old lady says
her mother came to London,
saw the wildflowers blooming
in the broken walls.
   Yes, light from darkness. Time
   to start afresh. We must
   forgive. Though not forget.

April, London

In Mile End Park the daffodils
explode again and he's beside me

telling how they're good as any
fringed the edge of Ullswater.

He talks about the beautiful,
the way it is inseparable

from the brutal. Think, he says,
the ghostly language of the earth:

its cresting waves: such majesty—
and threat. Its mountain peaks—reminders

of our frailty. And yet—
this splendid, fluttering host!

                      I think

the splendid, serried ranks that roared
at Nuremberg and prophesied

the bones and blitzmuck of this bombsite
underneath our feet. But yes,

they're beautiful and good as any
trimmed the banks of Windermere

that spring that year. Or any year,
whatever bad our futures bring.

Those First Evenings

Kitchen chairs and cupboards decompose
to obscure shapes, a shelf of dinner plates

is holding out against the creeping dark
that gathers strength in corners. At the table,

cup untouched beside him, evening paper
spread out, he is reading, unaware

a page has fallen to the floor. Is reading,
knows that night is nearly here. Is reading

and not reading. Pouring tea, and letting it
grow cold and sometimes glancing up, expecting

she might enter, arms full, laughing,
raindrops in her hair, the washing saved.

Chestnut Gathering

for Síle and Caitríona

Beside the Spa Hotel the chestnut trees
disrobe for winter. Two small girls on hands
and knees search silently intent until
the silken kernels snuggle in their palms.

Perched high above, a red-black eye slants sideways,
gusts of wind bring several soft thuds:
my two small girls split swollen pods, reveal
the shining, oily, unguent pearls inside.

Unsettled on his branch he lifts his beak,
twists broken song around a ragged theme
of satin skin grown coarse with age, like chestnuts
left aside to wrinkle out the years.

The old hotel veranda, ornate, glassed,
is shelter for two girls who count their spoil:
smooth chestnuts born of ancient, rain-soaked trees
and gnarled bark and soft October days.

Suburban Romance

for Kathy

It's our old car that suddenly fills
the front-door window. It's your yale key
metalling in the lock: "I'm home!" It's all
our talks together late at night while you
sat, sipping tea and listening patiently
to all my tedious tales out of school.

It's bric-à-brac we cannot bring ourselves
to throw away—a row of plastics bags
that waits around the corners of our lives
because there's nowhere else to put them, no
collection that will take them. Only someone—
years hence—who will hire a skip.

This house we filled with family—now filled
with just ourselves—looks after us. The garden
that I cleared of builders' rubble, that you
filled with roses and nasturtiums, blooms
again each year, unbidden and abundant.
Bills address us by a single surname.

Partner, colleague and significant other;
spouse, amanuensis, missus, sidekick,
boss and better half and other half
and special person; hand that rocked the cradle,
friend in need and deed, collaborator,
loyal and trusted confidant. The loved one.

II

... and
always embrace things, people earth,
sky stars, as I do freely and with
the appropriate sense of space ...

Frank O'Hara

This Turning Hour and Everything Intent

on furnishing another day, I see
a flake of sunlight slant from branch to leaf,
and raindrops wink among the clothes-pegs.

On the cobwebbed grass still wet with dew
a plastic laundry basket spills its colours,
ivy writes illuminated text

that tells how night is trembling on the cusp
of morning, blade and bark awakening
and every moment dying towards the dawn.

Back

There is a poem I said I would write
when I got out of hospital. Nothing too fancy.
Something about the flowers by the paths in the park—
    but I cannot block out those long corridors
    and the nurses' stations.

In the poem I would visit the corner shop
and look at the magazine rack with the pictures
of TV celebrities smiling, so happy—
    but all I can see are the posters explaining
    the dangers of smoking.

The poem would have said it was good to be back
in my housing estate with its rows of semis
and neatly clipped hedges and quizzical cats—
    but I cannot stop seeing my neighbours in beds,
    hooked up to machines.

The poem would have shown how people come home
in the evening from work and stand at their doors
for a few minutes' chat about football or prices—
    but all I can I hear are the nurse and the surgeon
    discussing my chart.

It was a poem that I needed to write
about so many things I thought I had lost,
a poem to describe how it feels to be back
    in an ordinary life. A poem to give thanks.
    And I do. I do.

Survivor

Driving down the Belgard Road
I see again the gossamer evidence
of my sitting tenant, snug
behind the glass of my wing mirror.

Rare the glimpse I've had of him
the time we've been together, I
so sure the wind would put an end
to his arachnoid acrobatics

but this tiny wight is match
and more for zippy morning breezes,
keen as elephant or moose
or mouse (or me) to cling to life.

In dead of night and lit by streetlamp,
undisturbed by prowling cat
or busy milkman he will toil
to realign his damaged webwork.

Then, come day, will venture out,
negotiate his deadly silk
to reach his breakfast, all the while
remembering to place his feet

along particular threads he spun
dissimilar from the others, ones
he left bereft of gum. But he
and only he, can tell which ones.

Material Support

He is come again to haunt the aisles,
so desperate his need. Come to inhale
the resin scent of deal and pine, planed
and unplaned pointing roofwards, waiting
for the mindful blade will recreate them
into shapes as yet still hovering ghostly
in his mind like Plato's caverned forms.
Again he wanders down long corridors
of paints and brushes, white electricals
and dazzling displays of indoor lights
that promise to undarken any soul,

surveys unsullied pruning shears and trowels
displaying gleaming edges, circular saws
and hand-tools nestling pristine in their boxes,
sharing side-by-side a universe
where every cordless drill will guarantee
its teethed chuck to grip the bit so tightly
that no tremble of the hand, no lapse
nor weakness in the aging brain will skew
the outcome. Who will pass these choirs of angels
shining in their tiers and not allow
he feels a sorrow lifting from his heart?

Others come with measuring tape and chart
and calculating eye and tilt of head
to weigh a purchase—motionless, he stands
in Fixings, undecided whether slot
or Philips screw or toggle-bolt or plug
would best secure a shelf to cavity wall
when suddenly the task appears before him
whole, its every separate part in place
and splendidly complete. And now he knows
that he can leave, depart as empty-handed
as the hour he entered, all his years ago.

Hymn

The kettle clicks to readiness.
The spoon reclines inside the mug
to hold the floating tea-bag down.
The milk jug stands at hand nearby.

The book remains unopened
on the bedside table, pencil
still alongside, glass of water
trembling, welcoming my step.

The washing flaps along the clothesline
firmly disciplined by pegs,
the garden shed keeps garden things
stowed safe behind its doors till spring.

Uncomplaining servants these
furnitures, appurtenances,
ministering to our needs and comforts,
loyal to the very end.

Who will send a broken chair,
a sagging bed, a shattered cup,
to swell the pitiless rubbish skip
without a stab of memory? Regret?

Longtime Companion

Beside the microwave
and Kenwood Chef and toaster—
me. There was a time

> you cupped your hands to drink
> freshwater from a stream,
> then had the sudden thought

to shape me. Later still
to round me on the wheel
and decorate me, bake me,

> sometimes accidentally
> break me in your earth-floored
> Neolithic kitchen.

And it wasn't long
before you learned to bend me
out of metal, came

> to place me in the graves
> of those who had departed
> for the Land of Shades.

These dials and switches now,
these interactive screens
and temperature controls

> are very welcome, but—
> always standing nearby
> full, or empty, me:

wooden, clay or metal,
porcelain or plastic,
ever I remain,

> Your humble servant.

The Safety of Numbers

How did they ever get around the world
with those old charts, our ancient mariners,
our bold explorers of the unknown vasts?
And did they think Herodotus had fixed
the boundaries with his two awkward lumps
depending south and east of Europe? Or
did Strabo ever lead a midshipman
to shout in loud excitement *Land Ahoy?!*

They'd heard reports of *terra incognita*
stretching from the horizon towards the rim
with monstrous creatures over-brimmed, and men
with heads that grew out of their armpits—
humanoid fantasticals described
by those who'd ventured—but not ventured far,
in holy fear of falling off the edge
and into God's great anger at impertinence.

Possessed by incoherent certainties,
unfazed by years of being disbelieved,
they sailed with little but their intuition
as their guide—as still it is with those
defy the safety of numbers, choose
to steer beyond the known with Erikson,
convinced that almost everything that leads
to anything worthwhile is wagered on a hunch.

The Stonemasons' Yard Revisited

(after Canaletto, The National Gallery, London)

Because I cannot pass where work is doing
these stonemasons busy at their craft
detain me, bell tower rising up behind them,
canal waters flowing silkily past.

I'd half-expected they'd have given way
to office-block and supermarket landscape,
but they labour still as first I saw them,
hammers poised to chip and split and shape.

Here's one who sculpts a column, narrowed eye
fixed on the point will take the chisel's edge.
Another decorates a pediment,
another finishes off a polished ledge.

And so much happening else outside their yard—
small cameos of ordinary lives:
a cockerel struts along a window sill,
a woman turns to help a fallen child,

while others set their lines of wash to dance
so whitely, merrily in the morning breeze—
their men will home this evening, tired and dusty,
must have shirts tomorrow fresh and clean.

No devil's workshops here, no idle hands
in this tableau of life and daily living:
his a world of stern allotted tasks
where all become what they are making, doing.

Poor Things

virginibus puerisque canto

Wednesday, period 2, Prescribed Poets—
and it's that great poem again: his *Stony Grey Soil*.
So many times I've read it out in class,
or asked some boy or girl to read it, listened
to their thick-tongued mumble, stumbling on words
like 'coulter'; tried to explain about bachelor farmers
and green-life-conquering ploughs. And I pitied them,
poor things.

Sometimes I played a recording, and they listened awhile
but drifted away to the disco tonight (by taxi,
not on bicycles two by two). Sometimes
I brought in a live poet, but they read out
in a reverent poetry voice, while I watched the sun
go down on my rows of freshly flowering faces
eying the school-room clock and pitying me,
poor thing.

That was the field where I worked to sow his wisdom,
daily reaping a crop of mobile phones,
of homeworks done under the desk for the next lesson.
And was my heart not badly shaken? Yes,
and often. But often again I would hear his laugh,
his whisper in my ear: 'Go easy, Master.
They too must spend their bright shillings of March,
poor things'.

American Diner

Looks like you could pick it up and move it
anywhere, some other town or city
if the business wasn't brisk enough—
could even plonk it on a movie set,
this self-contained American diner. Did it
make its way to Castleton, Vermont,
out of my torrid youth spent hanging round
with Mickey Spillane and Otto Preminger?

Inside, the scene is straight out of *The Killers*—
Are the cook and kid tied up together
in the kitchen? There behind the waitress
doing as she's told and 'acting normal'
as she lists me out the day's specials?
Which of those mean-looking guys who sit up
at the counter wait to nail the Swede?
And is that Dana Andrews sipping coffee?
Is that Alice Faye now swaggering over,
swivelling up beside him on a stool,
and showing off those great legs?

I take a seat along the window side
so's I can keep an eye out for James Cagney
who is keeping both eyes out for me
(a bit of money trouble, not to mention
Rita Hayworth) and who'll burst in
any moment looking for the rat
that double-crossed him, spot me right away
and pull his gun. There will be shouts and screams,
there will be frantic divings for the floor
but I've already seen his ugly mug
across the parking lot as he dodged in
and out between the Fords and the Buick Sedans.
What happens next sure won't be pretty. But

the eggs and bacon are delicious, pancakes
topped with maple syrup simply awesome.
And the waitress chatty with the refills,
business-like, her pencil in her hair,
her flirty quick-fire repartee amazing
and I have to say she's playing up
this walk-in, walk-off part so very well
she's bound to land a better role soon,
maybe something opposite Edward G?

And what's the story with that handsome guy
who took an end stool, leaving others empty
near the till?—I'd bet a couple of bucks
that he's a plain-clothes or a private dick
the way he has of leaning forward, peering
now and then across his paper. Bet
he's casing up the joint or watching someone?
That chap getting up to leave now?—Yep!
Handsome waits a couple of frames and then
he's stubbing out and strolling towards the exit,
right hand moving towards his right-hand pocket …

Now I'm on the run myself with Cagney
on my tail and tearing down the highway,
only one hand on the wheel, the other
shot to bits, blood everywhere, and wondering
how it was I got mixed up in this
when all I meant to say was—What a place!
Where anyone from anywhere (or even
anyone from any time) can walk in,
find that everything is just as was—
except in colour, not in black and white.
No suits or neckties, smart fedora hats,
but still the feeling if you took a stool
along the counter maybe Myrna Loy
would sit beside you, cigarette unlit
and giving you that look …

No, better not.
Just order coffee, try to shake the feeling
that you're just another extra, hired
to give this opening scene a bit of 'normal'
just before the door swings open, someone
tries to bolt and bullets ricochet—
Don't move! American diner sequences
are short, precursors to the car-chase.
Customers who keep out of the way
are safe. But still, it's best avoid the seats
along the counter. Take one by the window.
Watch the door …

In a Suburb of St Petersburg

Overwhelmed by The Hermitage,
its Watteau *fêtes galantes*, its Fragonards,
rococo *décoratifs* and droning guides—
we flee out to the suburbs on a tram.

Between apartment blocks, the evening sun
slants into narrow parks of patchy grass
where people sit, or loiter at the front
of ships' containers fitted out as shops.

A doorway frames us. Conversation halts.
We pause like newly landed cosmonauts
who hesitate to chance their next footfall.
We dare to try our meagre stock of Russian,

talk revives and gentle Lords and Ladies
elegantly posing on their lawns
are elbowed out as Brueghel dips his brush,
paints two more figures on a lively canvas.

Duende

So long a time can pass without a sign,
a sepulchral, endless silence undisturbed
until a morning bring the chirp of birdsong
and a rustling in the eaves. So long

a distant anvil rings and spits out sparks
until one flashes brighter than the rest,
illuminates the dark, like lines new-forged
that swell to sound and fill the soul with hope

as Zachariah was that morning filled
when Gabriel announced the barren years
were ended, life was quickening in the womb
where life so long a time had never stirred …

Prayer

Is there any way to claim back hours
when I was only technically living?
Hours accumulated in waiting rooms
with nothing but golf magazines for company?
A celestial credit-note might be issued, perhaps,
in lieu of tedious, endless odysseys
around the hinterlands of housing estates
before the bus-route finally reached my stop?

And all those wasted ages hunting car keys,
overdue library books, TV remote,
that other sock, the passport left in a place
where I would definitely find it next time.
Couldn't. Surely I am due a discount
for those phone calls kept me holding, trapped
inside interminable manglings of Mozart?
I beseech you, Lord, please hear my prayer.

On the Bus

Not my usual bus this—travelling
my accustomed route yes, but
taking in a few more twists and turns.
Look, that crumbling wall reveals a gap
I hadn't seen before; that gable end
extends a length back longer than I'd reckoned—
all these unfamiliar Roads and Groves
disclose a new perspective on old journeys,

like this morning that discarded notebook
found forlorning in a desk-drawer
and my half-hour spent deciphering
who was it wrote those hurried lines—who was it
tried to slow the world was whirling round him
faster than these neat suburban landscapes
racing past my window now? And yet
I knew of course that hapless wight was me.

This filtering of the ever-present past,
this yearning to go back, rein in the years
and speak a word to all those selves I was,
selves gauche and ill-advised and God knows what—
I want to shout to them above the maelstrom
swept me on relentlessly before it.
What the resurrections could be mine
if like to Hamlet's crab I could go backward?

Everything Must Go

Who had the heart to give away
these decorated tumblers? Not
regret the loss of this fine lamp?
Of these exquisite figurines
of shepherd boys and shepherdesses?
Surely there are necks would wear
these multicoloured necklaces?

The shelving bends with paperbacks,
and knick-knacks congregate in corners,
coats and jackets crowd the aisles
awaiting their deliverance—
like those poor souls in Purgatory
for whom we once were told our prayers
would gain a merciful release.

Theologies today are cool
about that region Dante painted
in such torrid colours but
the owner of this shop is not
so *Good News Bible* as he is
Old Testament Jehovah, fond
of fire and Judgments Final—Look:

out back, his plastic bags of stuff
that lingered too long on the rack.
Redemption here comes not through prayer
but ready cash. This cap, for instance,
shows the scars of wear but yet
still cuts a dash. Deserves reprieve.
Three Euro? Yes. I'll take it.

III

*... the wound
that will never heal right, will always have
a fat and tender scar, and will tear open
every day ...*

MATT W. MILLER

Migrant

Over tea and sandwiches
he talks about Romania,
and all the clubs he used to play for

back when times were better. Lean
and handsome in that Georgie Best way
you could see him dodge defenders,

dash into the six-yard box
to intercept a cross, strain up
to meet it. Hard at work again,

he digs outside our kitchen window,
flings up wintery lumps of clay,
his breath a rising fog around him,

every move mechanical
until he rests his spade and stares
beyond the garden, sees the half-chance

falling towards him, sees the goalie
stumble, feels the smack of leather
on his forehead. Hears the roar.

Threnody

I.   *Life Worth Living*
     On viewing old photographs of 1950s Manchester

Again I'm searching for you, this time
here in these old photographs
of Ancoats, Salford, Mexborough
and Moss Side—the Manchesters
that franked the postage on your letters
all those years you were away
from us, those places I have said
I'll visit someday to placate
my ghosts but know I never will.

I move among the Irish families
pictured living in damp rooms,
with broken windows and cracked walls
and grimy children holding dogs
up to the camera. I peer
at groups of men who stand on corners,
try to find a half-profile
that might be yours among them, laughing
in that boyish way you had.

There must survive some shade of you,
some faint imprint was caught in passing,
some blurred image of your face
agrime with coal dust, jacket wet
with rain—that figure there now, hunched
while lighting up a cigarette,
his left hand sheltering the flame—
but no. So desperate my pain
I see you everywhere. I see you

walking up these narrow streets
past back-to-back pit housing, slagheaps,
gaunt pit-head machinery
that looms against the skyline—see you

everywhere since I began
to have family of my own
and life began to tell me how,
had you returned to us, our lives
had been worth so much more the living.

II. *An Emigrant's Return*

A story from the Ireland of the 1950s

i

You stole tobacco from your father's coat
you told me, when he stumbled in at night.
You smoked it on the way to school next day.

Your lunch was milk with cuts of bread and porridge
and you found the reading and the writing
hard, but loved the songs. At fourteen years

you packed your bag and fiddle, took the boat
and joined your brothers, made your first descent
inside the cage and heard the cables straining

overhead. You prayed, you told me, prayed
The Sacred Heart would keep you safe from harm
and bring you back up from the dark again.

ii

I sit beside you in this hospital ward
remembering a youthful, jovial man,
dressed fashionably in the style of Orson Wells

or Joseph Cotton, Player's Navy Cut
between his fingers, laughing with his children,
lifting them above his head ... but then

another shade arrives, a man embattled,
bitter at the endless queuing up
for casual labouring work on building sites

that lasted just a month or two, or less,
and cursing Union rules and regulations—
Only Paid-up Members Need Apply.

iii

I watched you sit in moody silence, listened
while you sneered about 'our native land'
and how it's not the what you know but who

and how they told you, no, there's nothing here
for you now, Eddie. Nothing. Best go back
to where the work is. You'll be better off.

And so, more casual labouring, odd-jobbing,
doing gardens, selling door to door ...
I'd rather work a thousand miles below

than waste my time like this. And then the suitcase
standing in the hallway, awkward hugs
and *I'll be back before you know I've gone.*

iv

For days a quietness hangs about the house
and settles like a dust on everything.
I find a shaving brush, a set of darts

and once some cigarettes I try to smoke.
And then, the letters stamped in Lancashire
or Wales: *I'm in good digs. The work is hard*

but there is plenty of it. There is men
from every part of Ireland here. And then
the laboured writing telling clumsily

of love and how *we'll see each other soon*
at Christmas (or at Easter, Summer). *Sure*
it won't be long but I'll be home again.

Again, but different every time you came.
You'd shake my hand, and rough my hair and ask
if I was doing well at school? I'd blush

and lie. You'd stay at home a couple of nights,
and then a friend would call and you'd be off
to play your music in the noisy pubs

my mother hated and the 'coming home'
became another one or two-week visit
from your world of colliers and mineshafts,

Irish pubs and Irish music, dance halls,
sparsely furnished rooms and letters written
to a growing family of strangers.

Nothing else for men like me to do
but take the boat and sell the only thing
they've got. No need to look for favours though

or beg for work. Get up and dress and eat,
go down the pit, come up and wash and eat
go down the pub till midnight. Thousands like me,

tens of thousands crowding every night
in every public house in Manchester,
invited back to celebrate 'An Tóstal'—

Yes, 'The Emigrants' Return': come all ye
back and spend your money here in Ireland,
then go back to England, where you belong.

And later, when your lungs were choked with coal dust,
you still played your jigs and reels in pubs
until the night you stumbled in the street.

An emigrant myself, I went to see you—
someone I felt duty-bound to visit:
distant relative from a distant past.

It's in my mind a long time how I saw you
shuffling down the hospital corridor,
unsteady, one hand palmed along the wall.

I didn't know to call you 'dad', or 'father'—
you had passed before I said your name.
It's in my mind a long time your blank stare.

viii

This Dublin hospital where they shipped you back
was just a building site last time you saw it,
body strong enough to carry bricks.

I wanted that we'd talk about the years
we were together, those few early years
before the watching for the postman,

the listening for the wire-boy. Tell me,
in those final days you lay there, silent,
did you take the cage again each night,

descend the darkness, find the family
you had before the cables snapped, and you
were lost to us and we were lost to you?

III.   *My Father Saved Lives*

> On viewing the 'Chasing the Cure' exhibition
> at the Albuquerque Museum, New Mexico.

What scraps I have of you could fit
inside this cup in this café
in this museum in Albuquerque.

Dark, in that grey overcoat
your emigrant generation wore,
you come to me in troubled sleep,

your suitcase heavy by your side,
and sit down on my bed and speak,
but I can't hear you.

                              I remember

when you spent a summer working
on that site in Blanchardstown—
that sanatorium would save lives—

and told me how you built verandas
for the stricken to survive,
like these wan people photographed

a century ago, diseased
and exiled from the fetid East
to breathe New Mexico's crisp air,

do battle with the vicious daemon
that would later do for you.
That memory of that summer and you

building something would save lives
remains a tiny pinpoint, flickering
in the dark you left behind.

Bradley

One of your father's sisters married him.
Which one?—we clamoured, though we didn't know
one from another. The one that emigrated
to America. Now go out and play.

He disappointed us. America.
America. But he was short and stout
and looked like Mr Brown, our grocer.
And the way he spoke we thought was funny.

He drank his tea and talked a little of his loss
and how she'd always wanted they'd come over.
We sniggered at the way he said *'You bet'*,
'Gee whiz', like people in our comic books.

We played along the sidewalk at the bus stop
while he talked with mam. The *sidewalk*: his word.
Drugstore too. And when he shook our hands
he *reckoned* we might meet again sometime.

For days we played The American Visitor,
invented words he'd say, mimicked his voice,
grew tired of him, forgot him. Were surprised
when Christmas brought a doll, a cowboy suit.

Poem for a Young Religious

d.1905, aged 27 years, interred
at Mt Olivet Cemetery, Washington DC

Who were you, Sister, Irish name on stone?
What were those four years, virginal and veiled
until the hour when you began your vigil
underneath this cross, awaiting Gabriel?

What were your days until at twenty-three
you held the candle, took the ring, abjured
the life of Mary Durcan to become
this Sister Benoite de la Providence?

Sister Benoite de la Providence,
did you sincerely hold this hurried world
a trial to earn the joys of one to come?—
believed that we are not just flesh and bone

but souls struck from the anvil of creation,
sparks to light the darkness for a moment
before guttering into immortality?
A noisy traffic fills the nearby highway,

busier now than on the day you vowed
obedience, than on that final day
you made a last confession, were forgiven
and absolved—although it must have been

that you were innocent of mortal sin
and all but the most venial of the venial.
What led you to a life of abnegation?
What brought you to elect for servitude?

Speak to our condition now, allow us
understand devotion. Sacrifice.

IV

... a multiplicity of life
just outside the range of our perception,
always a glimmer at the edge of vision,
like the gleam of phosphorescence
off the boat's wake ...

CAROLYN L. TIPTON

Before the World Was Storied

(from the photography of Martin Jakubik)

This might be Charon's fateful keel
aground on Lough na Fuaiche's strand

and Midas must have touched this field
around the church at Ballyfanagh.

Beams laid bare by Rosbeigh's tides
allow us read a tragic tale,

these trees at Monasterevin sigh
faint echoes of St Eimhin's bell.

We give to every cairn its myth,
its legend every cromlech, lios—

but long before we entered time,
before we built at Poulnabrone

these waters mirrored primal skies,
split rivered fissures out of stone.

History

Montaigne retells Herodotus:
how Psammenitus did not weep
for son or daughter but for friend—

thus trickles down the centuries
the fall of Egypt's Royal House,
the humbling of a powerful king.

At Lucan Bridge this moment now
the river overcomes the weir
and carries leaves and twigs downstream.

Part of this surge perhaps the tears
of Psammenitus that inclined
Cambyses to be merciful?

And could this line of swans that pass
beneath these overhanging branches
trace a lineage back to Lir?

Trackway

Keenagh, Co. Longford, c.148 BC,

Eamhain Mhacha's fame was spreading,
Royal Cruachan Aí expanding
when this timber corduroy track
was laid across these ancient wetlands.

Here, the heavy work of those
who felled the several hundred trees
and those who strained to load the carts
and haul them creaking to Corr Liath.

Here, the skill of carpenters
split trunk with axe and shaped with adze,
and here the twist of dextrous fingers
wove the beds of brushwood mats.

These mortised joints with tenons tongued
to lock exactly one to one
were honed before the Inca masons
paved the Andean trails with stone.

A muffled sound of wooden cartwheels
seems to echo from these logs,
and thud of shaft-hole tool to linger
on the silence of the bog.

Loher

Co. Kerry, c.800 AD

Of you, our early Christian kin
who built this windswept fort as they
your ancestors in their bronze times
designed, we ask: what was your sort
that locked together stone to stone
around your dwellings, sent these stairways
spiralling up to battlements?

Fear crouched along these walls each night
till dawn allowed the eye to scan
for sail and coruscate of sword
might round the slant of Skellig Michael,
bring the slaver's yolk or slaughter
to this circular redoubt—
our only cypher of your stay.

Despite whatever might befall,
you fashioned out of rock a construct
fit for life above survival:
paved your drains, sank souterrains
would hide your loves come wrack of war,
come peace would store your food, keep cool
your wines came all the way from Spain.

Azulejos

Old men chat together in the shade
and sip their beers and watch the eager tourists
brave the heat to photograph these tiles
designed to baulk the savage midday sun.

Rectangles frame triangles, interlock
with squares, repeat themselves in patterns
devoid of human figure or divine,
as laid down strictly in the Prophet's laws—

until by force arms Queen Isabel
declared her Christian kingdoms purified
and Blessed Virgin Marys, Lambs of God
and other of the re-established Faith

appeared above the doors and lintels. But
the Azulejos hold their place, survived
time's never-ending storms to lend
material support to heavenly favour.

Nazca

I will never need to venture
past the Pillars of Hercules

Three storeys high, another world
hoves into view: birds' nests reveal
tight architectures, vagrant weeds
inhabit corners, playing fields
display white geometric lines
and ventilator shafts converge.

No daring voyage beyond the rim
will take me to more curious regions

Seen from here, a wondrous realm
of flat roofs trapping rainwater
and mirroring the infinite—
a world as strange and unfamiliar
as the windswept plains of Mars,
or valleys under Venusian cloud.

I never linger on this stairwell
but, transfixed, recall again

the Pampas de Jumana carved
with giant figures: hummingbirds
and snakes, invisible from below—
a landscape Sir John Mandeville
might have described. And runways laid,
it's said, to welcome back the Gods.

A New England Schoolroom c.1845

Each day I write a headline on the blackboard
which the children copy neatly in their books.

> *Say well is good,*
> *do well is better*

In this one-room school I spend my years
and pace its wooden floor, peer out its windows.

> *One today*
> *is worth two tomorrows*

A savage race, I teach, once walked these paths
that we've made roads. Were ignorant of His name.

> *It's not how long*
> *but how well we live*

Each year I watch the leaves flame into fall
and listen to them rustling on the shingles.

> *We do not fear tomorrow*
> *for God is always there*

In winter, with one stove to fight the cold,
the snows will often empty out my classroom.

> *Only virtue*
> *is the true nobility*

Spring and summer and then fall again:
another row of children memorising:

> *After all is said and done,*
> *more is said than done*

He led us here, I teach. Made manifest
our destiny. Our New Jerusalem.

Vermont, USA

The Liberation of Tibet

On the streets of Lhasa's New Town,
noisy traffic, glassy shops
and neon signs and all the best
of brands: Bugatti, KFC.
And smiling, helpful people wanting
to speak English. Muffled shouts
of soldiers marching in the barracks
left and right and left and right.

And many more of welcoming Han
than grave Tibetans until New Town
fades to narrow lanes and stalls
and multi-coloured flags that wave
above the Jokhang Temple. Monks
chant loud above the megaphones
of Chinese tourist guides who try
to summarise the Pratimoksha.

Regal on its clouded heights
the white Potola Palace, splendid
as the time Younghusband pillaged,
as the time Mao's youthful zealots
vandalized its sacred treasures.
Pilgrims in the streets below
prostrate themselves, fulfil the Kora,
hand-boards rasping on the pavements.

Minimarkets all agree
that visitors must have Cornflakes,
the bookshops offer histories
of subjugations past. A sculpture
in the central square proclaims
the socioeconomic gains
since first the People's Army wrought
the Liberation of Tibet.

Black Rat Replies

Collection boxes are out again
to save the cuddly panda bear
and leaping antlered antelope.

No rattling of the box for me.
It's said, together with the flea,
I almost wiped out human kind,

although, unlike benighted creatures
trembling towards extinction, there
is something in the loggers, poachers,

drillers-down-for-oil defies
the odds. The question's often put:
what greater good had He in mind

to have me in His scheme of things?
What do I add to His designs?—
Not for me to answer, but

to say there is a killer species
He inflicted on the world
the which the world could do without.

Disasters

Poem dedicated to the man who found his car
clamped and complained that it was 'a disaster'

Damocles knew how frail the thread
but Saki caught the sniper's bullet
urging others to be careful

and St Ruth astride at Aughrim,
giving orders, never saw
the cannonball took off his head.

That pleasant Ache afternoon
its people did not understand
the towering wave would overwhelm them

and remember how in Paris
Roland Barthes stepped into traffic,
died in hospital days later?

Dionysius played a cruel jest
but Damocles could see the blade
that dangled overhead, just as

enforcement of the parking laws
is something not quite unexpected,
not completely down to Fate

whereas disasters come to us
unheralded and strip us bare,
are pitiless and coffin-shaped.

20 July 1969 AD

'May the spirit in which we came
be reflected in the lives of all mankind'

When we pressed our footprints on your crust
we trod on centuries of endless yearning,
long fragmented into silvery dust,

> *O Queen of Tides*

remembered verses of old songs and rhymes
addressed to you by poets who disturbed
your tranquil seas with sad despairing lines

> *Nightfarers' Guide*

and when we walked the pock-marked desert plains
our mediaeval ancestors believed
were gouged to show the murderous shape of Cain

> *Translucent Lantern*

and sank our probes into your soil to gauge
was Beatrice right to hold the dark spots equal
to the bright and not more dense or rare,

> *Latona's Child*

and sent back images of figures lumbering
towards a distant hill where high beyond
the outline of a dry horizon's rim

> *Apollo's Kin*

we saw our troubled homeland poised above us,
viridescent oceans veiled in cloud,
and felt this day must herald Pax Lunaris.

Three Homilies

For these times

I. Lamentations 5:17

The radio talks of peace again:
peace talks intensify. And so
that must be good, I think, and pause
and take a quick look-in on her:
The radio says there's peace talks. But
she doesn't answer, pulls the quilt
above her head and turns away.
Poor thing.

I close the front door carefully,
allow the broken lock to catch.
She'll be alright an hour or so.
No lift again. I take the stairs.
The cold seems worse against the *crump!*
and *crump!* continually getting nearer.
But there's talks. They say peace talks
intensify.

The people early bound for work
in Kramatorsk push bicycles
across the snow and war is war
but still the world must spin. I talk
and everybody talks and talks
of peace talks, how they've heard it said
peace talks intensify. And then
I see my neighbour

well wrapped up in that black coat
she bought last week, her bag held tightly
in that way that women do,
the way I saw her yesterday
and stopped, shocked. But no tears
today. I hurry past. Someone
has thrown a cloth across her face.
Poor soul.

Tonight the TV news will show
those grim-faced men around that table
we have seen so many times,
so many times before. Peace talks
intensify—but no agreement.
This is why our hearts are sick;
this is why our eyes are dim ...

II. The Book of Judges, 5:28

When will the car arrive, the uniforms
step out? For that will be the last time
I will sit here with Sisera's mother,

waiting, hoping, praying that our vigil
conjure them alive from Homs, Aleppo,
or the slaughtering in the Jezreel Valley

where the Israelites came to stain
Mount Tabor with their enemy's blood.
Did spear or sniper's bullet fell our sons?

The centuries between us have dissolved:
the countless battlefields become as one.
Why so delayed the hoofbeats from his chariot?

III.   The Revelation to John, 16:18-19

A rush of moccasined feet,
a crash of Aztec temple,
bright canisters of Zyklon
neatly stacked and shelved
and ready for action—
                              Look:
a flash of shield, of sword,
of Tomahawk missile—
Tasmanian warriors whisper
and Crusader knights

71

rampage and pillage—
                    See:
a storm lets loose its lightning
over Wounded Knee
and Alexandria;
destroys Aleppo, Dresden,
Cuzco, Carthage—
                    Hear:
a violent earthquake worse
than any ever was
since man first came to be.
Whole islands disappear
and the cities of the nations collapse.

06 August 1945 AD

That Monday morning he came early,
hoping to avoid the queue.
The Bank was still not open, though
he saw inside some clerks at work.

His watch said 8.15. He sat down
on the steps, then heard some noises
overhead, saw... parachutes? Yes,
parachutes descending. Strange,

so early in the morning—this
his final thought but one, which was:
they take their time these bankers. And then
suddenly everything went white.

We know that he was there that morning
from his shadow printed neatly
on the steps. That stuff about
his thoughts I just made up because

it's what I might myself be thinking,
sitting there and waiting, worrying
would I yet again be late
for work in downtown Hiroshima.

Selfie

Wedged inside the morning crush
I read across a shoulder: POPSTAR
CELEBRATES HIS BIRTHDAY. FIREMEN
RESCUE KITTEN FROM A TREE—
and jammed between the horoscopes
and hair restorers (guaranteed):
the grainy image of a dawn
three hundred million miles away.

The camera arm has twisted back
to photograph the landing craft
that gleams despite its seven months
of surfing on the infinite,
while in the corner of the shot
and barely struggling into view
a land of dusty plains awakes
to skies of red and russet hue.

We hurtle underneath the Thames
from London Bridge to Baker Street,
imprisoned in the warp of space,
the granularity of time
that scores and shapes the universe …
but now the page is turned again—
I scan the TV lists and—Yes!
We're DANCING WITH THE STARS tonight!

26 November 2018

Now the Gods Are Gone,

our great lawgivers fled,
portentous statues toppled,
smashed and spilling nothing
but the hollowness
we long suspected—now

the vast elysian fields
were promised us flattened
into car parks, endless
supermarket forecourts,
urban sprawls—and now

the things eye hath not seen
nor ear heard are replaced
by concrete, glass and plastic,
we must cut our clothe
and be content with carpet

underfoot, enjoy
the satisfaction got
from quality goods discounted,
guaranteed top-class
or money back. Now that

the fickle gods are stripped
of godliness, our martyrs
fools, Olympus nothing
but extinct volcano,
Jove and Jesus banished,

we must find salvation
in our earthly comforts:
colour-coded bathrobes,
matching patterned curtains,
bought on clearance. Now

the gods have vanished,
their sanctifying graces,
miracles, rewards
and punishments suspended,
we must turn to bargains

in the here and now,
divine our happinesses
best we can with savings
gained at cut-price shops
purveying one-day-onlys.

See the Many Mansions
up for Immediate Sale
(in need some repair)—
excrescenting among
the gleaming new apartments.

On Arriving into a Great City in March,

the new year gathering speed the more
the highway slows beside the track, the more
the overpasses criss and cross above us
and the hours we've left behind become
a coupled mass, the more the concrete sleepers—
long a blur that paralleled our journey—
now emerge each one a single cast,
the more the train slows towards our destination.

Gantries overhead dictate directions,
road signs peer from parapets and railings,
indicating yields-of-way and turns-off,
warnings how a moment's hesitation
can de-rail a life was inattentive,
satisfied to coast along as we now,
clattering through a narrow tunnel, faces
painted by a yellow light and sliding

smoothly towards the city while the month
accelerates and rises like an aircraft
soaring nose-up out of sight—our March,
the month that sprang so quickly on us, month
remembers resolutions made, the month
reminds us that the year is new no longer,
sparks unease, a need to sort things out,
to do whatever was we said we would.

Apartments eat the skyline, shops burst out
on corners, drivers caught in midday traffic
watch us watching them and know our months
and days and theirs are disappearing fast,
despite nomenclatures designed to hold them—
April looms, and May is up and yawning,
June's awake and all the calendar
astir and getting ready to bear down …

We rummage out our luggage, crowd the aisles,
impatient for the platform to stop moving,
resolute this time, this time we will.
No matter how intractable the present,
how encumbering the past, we will
lay hold of these last days of March, allow
no moment fall away from us unnoticed
once we foot the spinning earth again.

Inspirations

A POEM MUST: see Matthew 13:8-9; Luke 14:18-20.

I

The quotation is from Edgar Lee Masters' poem 'Ernest Hyde' in his *Spoon River Anthology* (1915).

HE WALKS HIS SEVERAL CITIES: The quotation ('Only in tradition is my love') is from Pasolini's 'Poesie mondane' ('Worldly Poems'), in which he also writes *'Mostruoso è chi è nato dalle viscere di una donna morta....'. (A monster is he born from the entrails of a dead woman...)* mourning the Rome he used to know. Walking in modern Dublin, I feel his sense of loss.

SIDE STREET: Tom Duddy's poem which I heard him read in 2011 at the launch of his collection The Hiding Place. When I read it now, I can still hear his soft, unassuming voice and his gift of finding the mysterious in the ordinary.

REMEMBERING TOM DUDDY: a tribute.

LEESON BRIDGE, EVENING: the smartly-dressed young people crossing Leeson Street Bridge in Dublin in the evening always remind me of my years as an office worker.

THE WHERE: written after reading Alan Bailey's heartrending book 'Missing, Presumed' (Liberties Press, 2014) which documents the disappearance without trace of six Irish women. There are of course many others, and worldwide.

REMEMBRANCE DAY: in a cemetery in Vermont, USA.

BLACK SATURDAY 1941 REVISITED: after a walking tour entitled 'Blitzed London.'

APRIL, LONDON: Mile End Park now covers one of East End London's most bombed areas during World War II. The interlocutor is Wordsworth who warned against having a twee view of Nature.

THOSE FIRST EVENINGS: On a neighbour's inconsolable grief.

CHESTNUT GATHERING: a snapshot of my two daughters when they were very young. The 'old hotel veranda' at the entrance to the Spa Hotel in Lucan is now much modernized.

SUBURBAN ROMANCE: a tribute to the woman who has been my patient and understanding wife/partner for such a long time.

II

The quotation is from Frank O'Hara's poem 'A True Account of Talking to the Sun at Fire Island', in *The Collected Poems of Frank O'Hara*, University of California Press, 1995.

THIS TURNING HOUR AND EVERYTHING INTENT: gratitude at being allowed another day.

BACK: after a narrow escape from the chap in the black cloak with the scythe.

SURVIVOR: on discovering a fellow combatant against mortality lodged in the wing mirror of my car.

MATERIAL SUPPORT: inspired by a lifetime of happy visits to DIY stores, now unhappily coming to an end.

HYMN: praise for the everyday supports we take for granted.

LONGTIME COMPANION: tribute to a menial piece of kitchenware, long a contributor to our material support and well-being.

THE SAFETY OF NUMBERS: dedicated to those people who always wait for others to stick their necks out before they themselves declare their views. If they ever do.

THE STONEMASONS' YARD REVISITED: A tribute to the wonderful canvas by Giovanni Antonio Canal ('Canaletto') which depicts people at work in the everyday life of Venice, c.1725.

POOR THINGS: the difficult experience of teaching Kavanagh's great poem of rural Ireland to city teenagers and of being rescued by his understanding of life. The quotation is from Horace: *I sing for girls and boys.*

AMERICAN DINER: a tribute to that iconic setting, a part of so many American gangster films. The great James Cagney *had* to figure.

IN A SUBURB OF ST. PETERSBURG: on the idea that it's acceptable to become weary of too much High Culture.

DUENDE: inspired by Federico Garcia Lorca's essay (*Juego y Teoria del Duende / Theory and Play of the Duende*) on, among other things, inspiration.

PRAYER: composed in a dentist's waiting room.

ON THE BUS: Bus journeys often occasion self-reflection.

EVERYTHING MUST GO: charity shops are places of redemption where objects get a second chance at life. Unlike us.

III

The quotation is from Matt W. Miller's poem 'Behold, Here is My Mark' in his collection *The Wounded for the Water*, Salmon Poetry, 2018.

MIGRANT: The past is always present.

THRENODY:
I.   *Life Worth Living*: a poem of yearning.
II. *An Emigrant's Return*: written out of the difficulties faced by Irish working-class families in the Ireland of the 1950s, and particularly by my own family during that time.
III. *My Father Saved Lives*: one of the early memories of my absent father that I cling to.

BRADLEY: an early memory of a family visitor from America and his loss.

POEM FOR A YOUNG RELIGIOUS: an attempt to get beyond the opprobrium now often shown for the religious life. Searching for family-related graves in Mt. Olivet Cemetery in Washington DC, I found a section of convent burials. One of the headstones bears the inscription: 'Sr. Benoite de la Providence. Little Sister of the Poor, *nee* Mary Durcan. d. Nov 20 1905. aged 27—Professed 4 yrs'. It brought to my mind all the Irish women religious who emigrated in the past and gave their life's work to teaching and medical congregations.

IV

The quotation is from Carolyn L. Tipton's poem 'Wishbone for the Millennium', in her collection *The Poet of Poet Laval*, Salmon Poetry, 2019.

BEFORE THE WORLD WAS STORIED: what was the world before we came along and obscured it with our myths?

HISTORY: concerning the unbroken chain of events that lead down to our own (short) day.

TRACKWAY: a tribute poem to our remote ancestors and their ingenuity at providing material support for human living.

LOHER: as 'Trackway' above. With wine.

AZULEJOS: good, practical ideas survive the worst of circumstances.

NAZCA: unremarkable landscapes reveal strange sights when viewed from above.

A NEW ENGLAND SCHOOLROOM C.1845: a blackboard in a schoolroom on display in the Shelburne Museum in Vermont shows a series of chalked admonitions, redolent of the times.

THE LIBERATION OF TIBET: inspired by the great changes brought about for the people of Tibet and their culture by The People's Republic of China.

BLACK RAT REPLIES: thoughts about which species has the most destructive presence on our planet.

DISASTERS: To do with inflationary misuse of words.

20 JULY 1969 AD: The sub-heading is part of the message on the plaque left on the moon by our intrepids. The hopes for Pax Lunaris remain unfulfilled.

THREE HOMILIES: three linked poems on the catastrophic intrusion of war into the daily lives of ordinary people and (in III) the apocalyptic end that many fear, despite the hope expressed in 20 July 1969 AD above.

06 AUGUST 1945 AD: The arguments continue: was it necessary?

SELFIE: news of extraordinary events is often swallowed up in the day-to-day.

NOW THE GODS ARE GONE: inspired by, and much inferior to, W.H. Auden's great 'Sob, Heavy World' in his The Age of Anxiety (1947)

ON ARRIVING INTO A GREAT CITY IN MARCH: Tempus fugit.

Acknowledgements

My gratitude to the editors of the following magazines and websites who first published these poems:

Ballyroan Public Library website, Dublin: 'Migrant'

Boyne Berries magazine, Co. Meath: 'A poem must'

Crannóg magazine, Galway: 'The Stonemasons' Yard Revisited' and 'Disasters'

Cyphers magazine, Dublin & *Domenica di Lettura* (online, Italy): 'This Turning Hour and Everything Intent'

FLARE, Dublin: 'Material Support', 'The Liberation of Tibet' and 'A New England Schoolroom c. 1845'

The Irish Times, Dublin: 'Before the World Was Storied' and '20 July1967 AD'

Lea Green Down: Anthology, Dublin, ed. by Eileen Casey: 'Poor Things'

Live Encounters on-line magazine, Ireland: 'Leeson St Bridge, Evening', 'My Father Saved Lives', 'The Safety of Numbers', 'Duende', 'Trackway', 'Black Saturday 1941 Revisited' and 'Longtime Companion', 'On the Bus', 'Black Rat Replies', 'Azulejos', 'Nazca', 'On the Bus', 'Everything Must Go'.

North West Words online magazine, Donegal: 'The Where' and 'American Diner'

Senior Times magazine, Ireland; *Domenica di Lettura* (online, Italy): 'April, London'

Shades of Scaldwood anthology, Dublin, ed. by Pat Quigley: 'Chestnut Gathering'

Skylight47 magazine, Galway: 'Survivor', 'In a Suburb of St. Petersburg' and 'Prayer'

Southword online magazine, Munster Literature Centre: 'Those First Evenings'

StepAway online magazine, UK: 'He Walks His Several Cities'

The Stony Thursday Book, Limerick: 'An Emigrant's Return'

Grateful acknowledgement also to Liz McSkeane, Anamaria Crowe-Serrano and Ross Hattaway of the Toika workshop.

Lastly and certainly not leastly my thanks to Jessie Lendennie and Siobhán Hutson Jeanotte of Salmon Poetry for enabling this collection to see the light of day.

EAMONN LYNSKEY is a poet and essayist. His work has appeared widely in leading magazines and journals and online. He has published three previous poetry collections: *Dispatches @ Recollections* (Lapwing 1998), *And Suddenly the Sun Again* (Seven Towers 2010) and *It's Time* (Salmon 2017). He was a finalist in both the Strokestown International Poetry Competition and the Hennessy Awards. A graduate of University College Dublin (BA), Dublin City University (MA), he also holds an M.Phil. in Creative Writing from Dublin University, Trinity College and a Diploma in Italian Language and Culture from the Italian Institute, Dublin. Before retirement he worked as a teacher and adult education director. He is a committee member and former Honorary Secretary of the Irish Writers' Union. More information available at www.eamonnlynskey.com

salmonpoetry
Cliffs of Moher, County Clare, Ireland

"Publishing the finest Irish and international literature."
Michael D. Higgins, President of Ireland